Complete Violin Sonatas and Trio Sonatas

ARCANGELO CORELLI

EDITED BY
JOSEPH JOACHIM AND FRIEDRICH CHRYSANDER

DOVER PUBLICATIONS, INC., NEW YORK

Published in Canada by General Publishing Company, Ltd., 30 Lesmill Road, Don Mills, Toronto, Ontario.

Published in the United Kingdom by Constable and Company, Ltd., 3 The Lanchesters, 162–164 Fulham Palace Road, London W6 9ER.

This Dover edition, first published in 1992, is a republication of Livres I, II and III of *Les Oeuvres de Arcangelo Corelli,* edited by Joseph Joachim and Friedrich Chrysander, and originally published by Augener & Co., London, n.d. [1888–90]. The German versions of Chrysander's prefaces have been omitted.

Manufactured in the United States of America
Dover Publications, Inc., 31 East 2nd Street, Mineola, N.Y. 11501

Library of Congress Cataloging-in-Publication Data

Corelli, Arcangelo, 1653–1713.
[Sonatas. Selections]
Complete violin sonatas and trio sonatas / Arcangelo Corelli ; edited by Joseph Joachim and Friedrich Chrysander.
1 score.
Op. 1–4 for 2 violins and continuo; op. 5 for 1 violin and continuo.
Reprints. Originally published: Les oeuvres de Arcangelo Corelli. Livres 1–3. London : Augener, 1888–1890.
Contents: Church sonatas in three parts, op. 1—Chamber sonatas in three parts, op. 2—Church sonatas in three parts, op. 3—Chamber sonatas in three parts, op. 4—Six violin sonatas, op. 5, part 1—Preludes, allemandes, correntes, gigues, sarabandes, gavottes, and follia, op. 5, part 2.
ISBN 0-486-27241-9
1. Trio sonatas (Violins (2), continuo)—Scores. 2. Sonatas (Violin and continuo)—Scores. I. Joachim, Joseph, 1831–1907. II. Chrysander, Friedrich, 1826–1901.
M178.C7S64 1992   92-14019
                                                    CIP
                                                    M

CONTENTS

TRIO SONATAS, OPP. 1–4

PREFACE

The first two volumes of Corelli's Works contain his 48 Sonatas or Trios—the compositions which first made his name celebrated. They came out in four parts, with twelve sonatas in each, thus: Op. 1, Rome, 1683[1]; Op. 2, Rome, 1685; Op. 3, Modena, 1689; Op. 4, Bologna, 1694. By reprints and copies they were reproduced in all countries with a rapidity never before known, and had a greater influence on the musical invention of their time than any other work of the same character. Op. 1 and 3 were intended for the church or for sacred concerts, Op. 2 and 4 for secular chamber performances, as is easily seen by the original titles, which are here prefixed to the several books.

These " Sonatas " form quartets for four instruments: Violin 1, Violin 2, Violoncello and an instrument of harmony, which in the sacred pieces is a theorbo[2] or organ, and in the secular a harpsichord. The bass part throughout this accompaniment is the same as the notes of the violoncello (or " violone " as Corelli still called it).[3] The chief differences between these two parts occur in Op. 1, in which for this reason the score is generally written on four lines. Otherwise only three lines were requisite; for the string bass, lute bass and accompanying bass are written together, and the performer must choose his own part from occasional hints (as _e. g._ on p. 168). In this matter the older music leaves to the performer a freedom unknown to the modern musician, yet necessary to be attained if he wishes to give life and brilliancy to his execution.

The figuring of the bass in the first Italian editions is rather less copious than in the present one, because I have availed myself of the additions made in the Dutch and English editions up to the year 1730, which give the chords fuller, without introducing any foreign elements into Corelli's harmony.

About the year 1725 an edition of these works was brought out by John Walsh in London, edited by Dr. Pepusch. However, it cannot be regarded as superior to the incorrect and careless English musical publications of that age, nor be treated as in any respect reliable.

FR. CHRYSANDER.

[1]Actually 1681.
[2]Corelli specifies the archlute rather than the similar theorbo.
[3]The violone and violoncello are not identical. The early editions of Corelli's sonatas actually specify the cello; only in a 1709 edition is the violone named as the bowed continuo instrument.

Church Sonatas, Op. 1

SONATA I.

Allegro.

SONATA II.

SONATA III.

SONATA IV.

Vivace.

Allegro.

Presto.

SONATA V.

SONATA VI.

SONATA VII.

SONATA VIII.

SONATA IX.

Adagio, e piano.　Allegro.

SONATA X.

Allegro.

SONATA XI.

SONATA XII.

Largo, e puntato.

unis.

Grave.

Allegro.

Chamber Sonatas, Op. 2

SONATA I.

Preludio.

Allemanda.

Largo.

Corrente.

Gavotta.

SONATA II.

Allemanda.

Corrente.

Allegro.

Giga.

SONATA III.

Preludio.

Largo.

Allemanda.

Adagio.

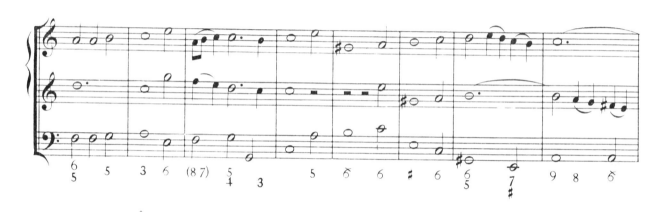

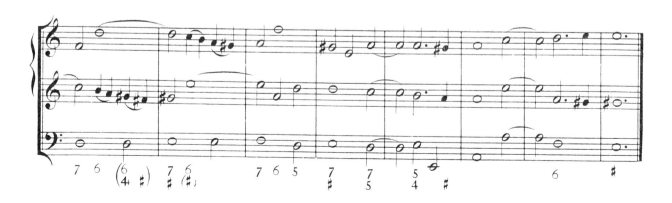

Allemanda.

SONATA IV.

Preludio.

Allemanda.

Presto.

SONATA V.

Preludio.

Sarabanda.

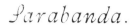

Tempo di Gavotta.

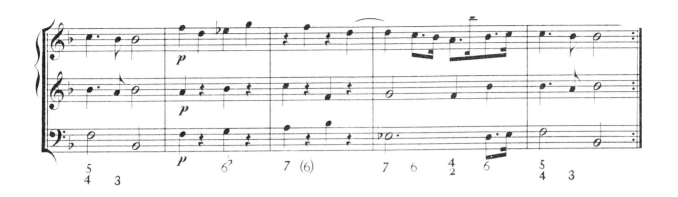

SONATA VI.

Allemanda.

Giga.

Allegro.

SONATA VII.

Preludio.

Corrente.

Allegro.

Giga.

Allegro.

SONATA VIII.

Preludio.

Tempo di Sarabanda.

Tempo di Gavotta.

Allegro.

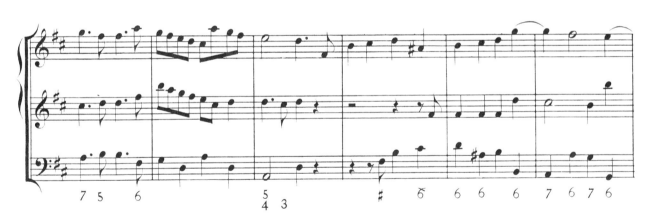

SONATA IX.

Allemanda.

Tempo di Sarabanda.

SONATA X.

Preludio.

Adagio.

Violino I.

Violino II.

Violone,
e Cembalo.

Allemanda.

Allegro.

Sarabanda.

Corrente.

SONATA XI.

Preludio.

Allemanda.

SONATA XII.

Ciacona.

Church Sonatas, Op. 3

SONATA I.

SONATA II.

Allegro.

SONATA III.

SONATA IV.

Adagio.

SONATA V.

SONATA VI.

Violino I.

Violino II.

Violone,
e Organo.

Grave.

Org.

SONATA VII.

SONATA VIII.

Allegro.

SONATA IX.

SONATA X.

SONATA XI.

SONATA XII.

Chamber Sonatas, Op. 4

SONATA I.

Preludio.

Corrente.

Allegro.

Allemanda.

SONATA II.

Preludio.

Allemanda.

SONATA III.

Preludio.

Violino I.

Violino II.

Violone
e Cembalo.

Corrente.

SONATA IV.

Preludio.

Grave.

Violino I.

Violino II.

Violone
e Cembalo.

Giga.

SONATA V.

Preludio.

Adagio.

Allemanda.

SONATA VI.

Preludio.

SONATA VII.

Preludio.

Grave.

Sarabanda.

Vivace.

SONATA VIII.

Preludio.

Grave.

Violino I.

Violino II.

Violone,
e Cembalo.

Allegro.

Allemanda.

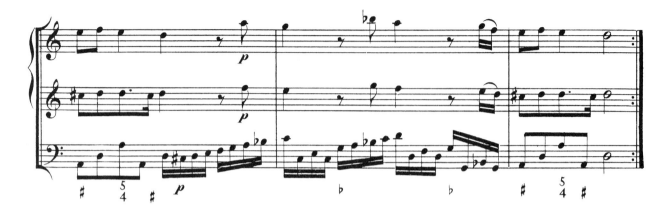

Sarabanda.

Allegro.

SONATA IX.

Preludio.

Largo.

Violino I.

Violino II.

Violone,
e Cembalo.

Corrente.

Allegro.

SONATA X.

Preludio.

Violino I.

Violino II.

**Violone,
e Cembalo.**

Grave

Presto.

Tempo di Gavotta.

SONATA XI.

Preludio.

Largo.

Corrente.

Allegro.

Allemanda.

Allegro.

SONATA XII.

Preludio.

Allemanda.

Presto.

Giga.

Allegro.

VIOLIN SONATAS, OP. 5

PREFACE

All Corelli's compositions succeeded in gaining popularity, and were thus circulated far and wide, and served as models for the musicians of his time; but the present *Opera quinta* was in this respect the most successful. It was taken up as a school-book in all countries; and if the copyright of our time had been valid then, Corelli would have grown rich even on the proceeds of this single work. But it yielded him something better than transient wealth, namely the renown of having founded the canonical work for the most valuable of stringed instruments.

Corelli published his work in Rome without indication of the place and without date, but from the dedication to Sophia Charlotte, Princess of Hanover, afterwards Queen of Prussia, we learn the year; the dedication is dated Jan. 1, 1700. As to the place, the Roman engraver Gasparo Pietra Santa is named. The work is divided into two parts with two title pages, as is shown in this edition.[1]

The first reprint seems to have been made in Holland, where the engraving of music on copper-plates was then brought to its greatest perfection, by Pierre Mortier of Amsterdam. To the fourth edition of this reprint we owe those additions which give the present edition a special value. These consist of the ornaments in the Adagios (very expressively called *graces* in English), which are by Corelli himself, for the title of Mortier's edition bears the words " Quatrième édition, ou l'on a joint les agréemens des Adagio de cet ouvrage, composez par Mr. A. Corelli, comme il les joue." It is to be inferred that the publisher obtained them from the composer direct or through the mediation of an artist-friend.[2]

John Walsh of London immediately made use of this enrichment of the favourite work, and published the graces, putting the same observation on the titlepage. However, in later editions he left them out, and I have not found them given again in any of the numerous reprints of the eighteenth century. The reason of this remarkable fact must be that they had not the same value for the practice of that age which they possess for us; for people did not wish to be tied to such ornamentation, even by the composer, since full freedom in these matters was allowed to the performer. It is known that others subsequently wrote graces and cadences to the pieces, which differed considerably from Corelli's; and for beginners and inexperienced players the master's own ornaments were neither intended nor suitable.

At the present day the matter is very different. To us Corelli's additions are invaluable as typical examples of a practice which has now gone completely out of use, but must be recovered if we are to thoroughly grasp the meaning of the music of his age and truly enjoy its rich treasures.

In Corelli's graces there occurs a small simple cross (+), which denotes a shake, longer or shorter according to the length of the note above which it stands. This indefinite cross, which appears also in Lully's opera scores with the same variety of meaning, was a French sign. The Italians marked shakes differently or else omitted them altogether. Consequently the cross cannot originate with Corelli, but must have been added by Mortier.

FR. CHRYSANDER.

Bergedorf near Hamburg,
    Dec. 1, 1890.

---

[1] The title pages have been omitted in the Dover edition, but the main titles are retained in the table of contents.
[2] The original publisher of these ornamented sonatas was apparently in fact the Amsterdam firm of Estienne Roger, whose edition Mortier seems to have pirated.

Violin Sonatas, Op. 5, Part I

SONATA I.

Allegro.

SONATA II.

SONATA III.

Corelli's Graces.

Adagio.

Violino solo.

Violone e Cimbalo.

Allegro.

SONATA IV.

SONATA V.

SONATA VI.

Corelli's Graces.

Violino solo.

Grave.

Violone e Cimbalo.

Allegro.

Preludes, Allemandes. . . . ,
Op. 5, Part 2

SONATA VII.

Preludio.

Corrente.

Sarabanda.

Largo.

Giga.

Allegro.

SONATA VIII.

Preludio.

Largo.

Violino solo.

Violone e Cimbalo.

Allemanda.

SONATA IX.

Preludio.

Largo.

Tempo di Gavotta.

SONATA X.

Preludio.

Allemanda.

Sarabanda.

SONATA XI.

Preludio.

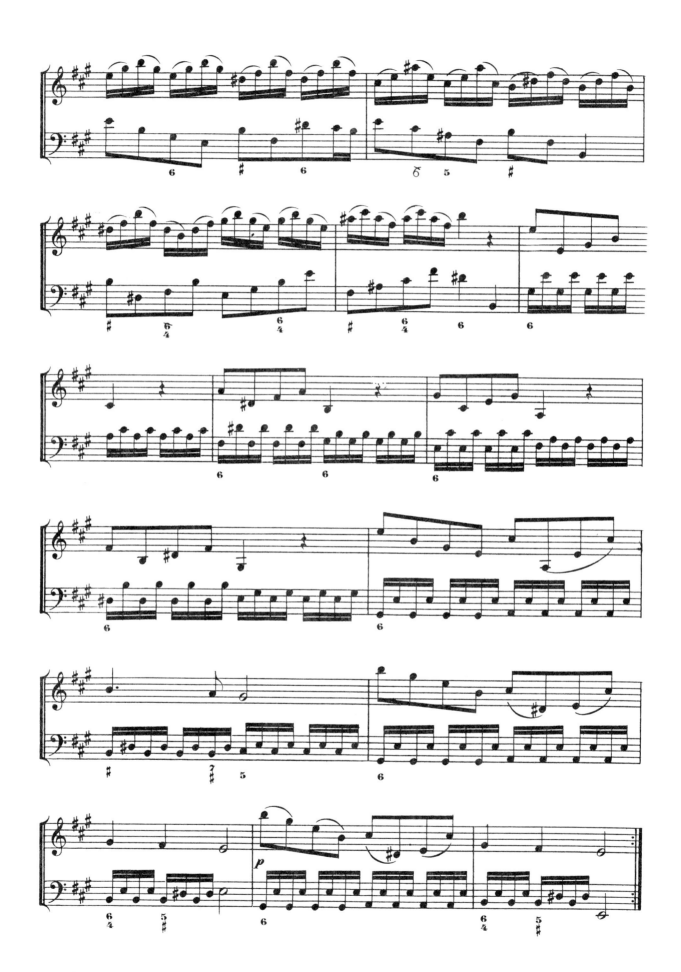

Gavotta.

Allegro.

XII. FOLLIA.

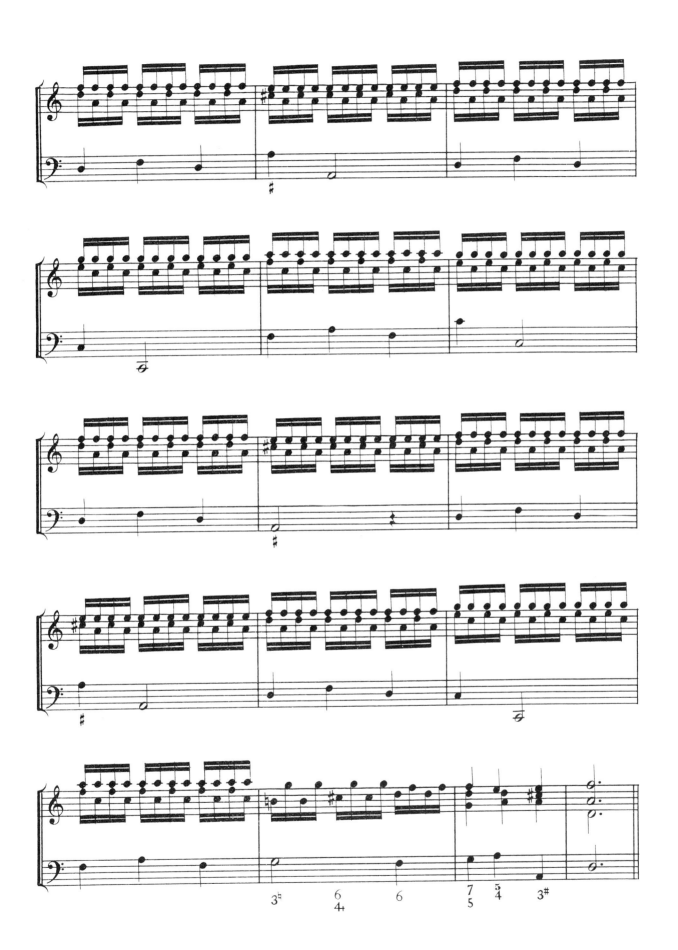

FINE.